Helen Keller

A Photo-Illustrated Biography

by Muriel L. Dubois

Consultant:
Keller Johnson-Thompson
Ambassador
American Foundation for the Blind

Bridgestone Books
an imprint of Capstone Press
Mankato, Minnesota

Bridgestone Books are published by Capstone Press
151 Good Counsel Drive, P.O. Box 669, Mankato, Minnesota 56002
http://www.capstone-press.com

Library of Congress Cataloging-in-Publication Data
Dubois, Muriel L.
    Helen Keller / by Muriel L. Dubois.
      p. cm.—(A photo-illustrated biography)
    Summary: A biography of Helen Keller, an author and activist for people with disabilities who was born in 1880 and lost her sight and hearing to an illness in 1882. Includes bibliographical references and index.
    ISBN 0-7368-1605-4 (hardcover)
    1. Keller, Helen, 1880-1968—Juvenile literature. 2. Blind-deaf women—United States—Biography—Juvenile literature. [1. Keller, Helen, 1880-1968. 2. Blind. 3. Deaf. 4. People with disabilities. 5. Women—Biography. 6. Sullivan, Annie, 1866-1936.] I. Title. II. Photo illustrated biographies.
HV1624.K4 D8 2003
362.4'1'092—dc21   2002009134

Editorial credits
Erika Shores, editor; Karen Risch, product planning editor; Linda Clavel, cover designer and interior illustrator; Alta Schaffer, photo researcher

Photo credits
Bettman/CORBIS, 14, 18, 20
Hulton/Archive by Getty Images, cover
Hulton-Deutsch Collection/CORBIS, 16
Patrick Hood/Colbert County Tourism & Convention Bureau, 6
Photos courtesy of Helen Keller Foundation, 4, 8, 10, 12

1 2 3 4 5 6 08 07 06 05 04 03

Table of Contents

"There are two worlds: the world that we can measure with line and rule, and the world we feel with our heart and imagination."
–Helen, in her book, *The Open Door*

Helen Keller

When Helen Keller was a baby, she became ill. The illness left her blind and deaf. Helen could not see or hear the world around her.

Helen's parents hired a teacher for Helen. The teacher taught Helen to communicate. Helen learned to share her ideas and feelings with the people around her.

As an adult, Helen worked to help others. She became an activist. Helen worked to change laws affecting people who are blind or deaf. She also raised money for the American Foundation for the Blind.

Helen was a writer. She wrote articles for magazines. She also wrote books about her life as a person who was blind and deaf.

Helen Keller traveled around the world. She became famous for her work for the blind.

Helen spent her life working for the blind.

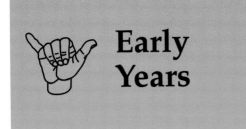

Early Years

Helen Adams Keller was born on June 27, 1880. She lived with her parents in Tuscumbia, Alabama. Helen had two older brothers and a younger sister. Her mother, Kate, cared for the home and family. Helen's father, Arthur, was a newspaper editor. People called Arthur Keller "Captain." He had served as a captain in the Civil War (1861–1865).

The Keller family lived on a small farm. The Kellers called their house and farm "Ivy Green." They grew cotton, vegetables, and fruit. They raised some farm animals.

Helen was a good baby. She liked to play. Helen could talk when she was six months old. She could say simple words like "tea" and "water." When she said water, it sounded like "wah-wah."

The Keller family lived on a farm called Ivy Green.

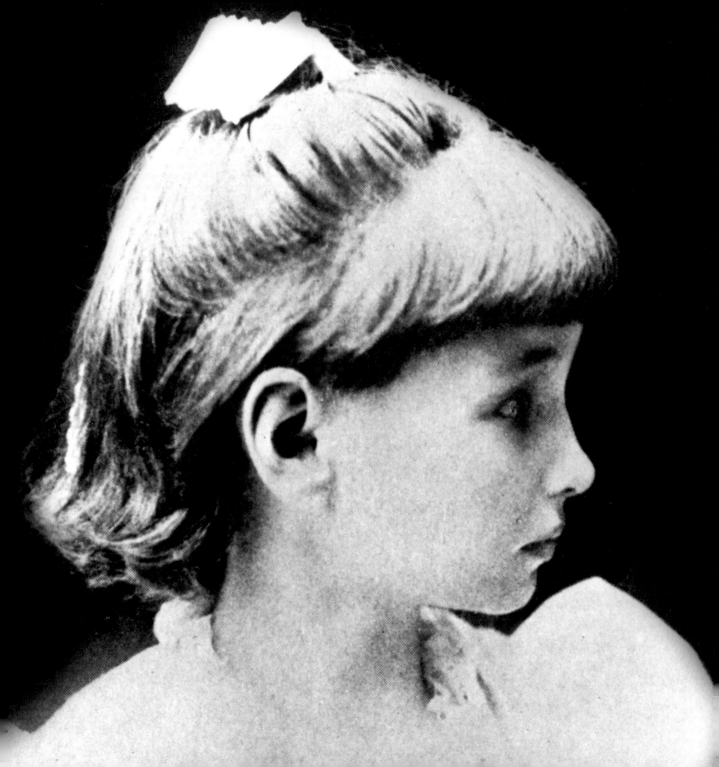

Helen Becomes Ill

In February 1882, Helen was 19 months old. She became ill with a very high fever. The doctor thought she might die. Finally, Helen's fever went away. She remained weak and slept much of the time.

One day, Kate moved her hand near Helen's eyes. Helen did not blink. Kate rang a loud bell near the baby. Helen did not move. Kate realized her daughter was blind and deaf.

Helen could not see faces or colors. She could not hear words or learn the names for things. The Kellers did not know what to do for their daughter.

As Helen grew older, she misbehaved. She had temper tantrums. She sometimes bit or pinched. The Kellers did not want to punish Helen. She did not know she was hurting anyone. She could not hear the other person cry or yell.

When Helen was very young, she often misbehaved because she could not tell people what she wanted.

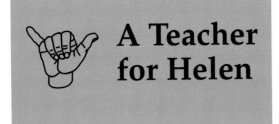

A Teacher for Helen

The Kellers wanted to help Helen. They knew Helen was smart. They wanted Helen to learn to be kind.

The Kellers wrote letters to many people. They asked about a teacher for Helen. The head of the Perkins School for the Blind in Boston wrote back. He knew the perfect teacher for Helen. Her name was Anne Sullivan.

Anne was blind as a child. An operation helped her to see. When Anne was blind, she studied at the Perkins School. She learned how to read braille. Braille is sets of raised dots on paper. Each set of dots stands for a letter. Blind people can read the letters by running their fingers over the dots.

Anne also knew American Sign Language (ASL). To use ASL, a person makes certain shapes with their hands. Each shape stands for a letter or word. A deaf person communicates with ASL.

People can read braille by running their fingers over raised dots.

Anne Sullivan

Anne met 6-year-old Helen on March 3, 1887. Anne gave Helen a new doll. Anne spelled "d-o-l-l" into Helen's hand. Helen copied the letters into Anne's hand. Helen did not know she was spelling a word. She thought she was playing a game.

Anne continued to spell words in Helen's hands. Helen copied Anne. Anne knew Helen had a good memory. She also knew Helen did not yet understand what their game meant.

Anne taught Helen to behave. Anne made Helen eat with her own spoon. She made her wash her hands at the pump. One day, while Helen washed, Anne spelled "water" into Helen's hand. Suddenly, Helen knew the signals in her hand stood for the water she was touching. She understood that everything had a name. Helen made Anne spell everything Helen touched.

Anne (right) taught young Helen how to communicate.

"In the wonderland of Mind, I should be free as another."
–Helen, in her book, *The Story of My Life*

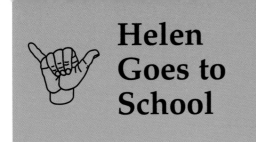

Helen Goes to School

Helen learned to name objects. She learned to spell sentences. Anne taught Helen to write. They used a special board with slits. Helen could put her pencil between the slits to keep her letters straight. Helen read braille books. She learned to read lips by putting her fingers on a person's mouth.

In 1888, Anne took Helen to the Perkins School. Helen loved the school. She met other blind children. Some children knew ASL and spelled into Helen's hands. Helen also learned to speak. A singing teacher helped Helen use her voice.

In 1896, Helen attended Cambridge School for Young Ladies. This school prepared Helen for college. She studied hard. In 1900, Helen was accepted to Radcliffe College in Massachusetts. With Anne's help, Helen graduated in 1904. Helen then wanted a job to earn her own money. She wanted to help others.

Helen graduated from Radcliffe College in 1904.

"I had overcome deafness and blindness sufficiently to be happy."
–Helen, in her book, *Midstream: My Later Life*

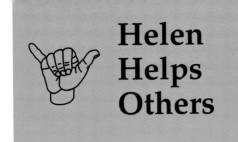

Helen Helps Others

Helen soon began working for the American Foundation for the Blind. People also asked her to work for the deaf. Helen did not think she could serve both well. Helen decided to focus on helping people who were blind.

Helen wrote magazine articles and gave speeches. She met with wealthy people. She asked them to give money to places that help blind people. She spoke to lawmakers. She asked them to think of how laws would affect the blind. She traveled throughout the world asking people to help the blind.

By 1914, Anne often was ill and needed help assisting Helen. They hired Polly Thomson as an aide. Polly went with Anne and Helen on their trips to other countries.

Helen wrote articles and speeches asking for help for the blind.

Movie Star

In 1918, Helen went to Hollywood, California. She starred in a movie about her life. It was called *Deliverance*. Anne and Polly told Helen what she needed to do in each scene of the movie. The movie's director stamped the floor so Helen would know when to perform her scenes.

From 1920 to 1924, Anne, Helen, and Polly traveled throughout the United States. They performed a show in theaters. In their act, they explained how Helen learned to communicate.

Other countries asked Helen to visit. She went to Europe. She visited Japan. Everywhere she went, Helen raised money for the blind.

In 1936, Anne Sullivan died. Helen missed her teacher, but she continued her work. Polly remained Helen's aide. Together, they continued to travel and speak about blindness.

Helen traveled around the world with the help of her aide, Polly Thomson.

"Through these dark and silent years, God has been using my life for a purpose I do not know. But one day I shall understand and then I shall be satisfied."
–Helen, in her book, *The Story of My Life*

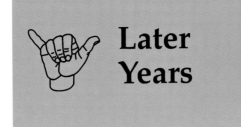

Later Years

Helen traveled around the world nine times during her life. She visited 35 countries.

During World War II (1939–1945), Helen visited wounded soldiers. She gave hope to men who had lost their sight or hearing. She continued to travel and raise money to build schools for the blind.

In 1964, President Lyndon Johnson gave Helen the Presidential Medal of Freedom. This medal is America's highest award for non-military people. One year later, in 1965, Helen was elected to the Women's Hall of Fame.

Helen spent her final years in Westport, Connecticut. She called her home "Arcan Ridge." Helen died in her home on June 1, 1968. She was nearly 88 years old. Today, many people continue Helen's work for the blind.

Helen lived in Connecticut at her home, Arcan Ridge, until she died in 1968.

Fast Facts about Helen Keller

 Helen appeared in two movies, *Deliverance* and *Helen Keller: Her Story*. She received an Oscar for the second film.

 Helen was able to read five different kinds of print for the blind, including American braille and European braille.

 Helen learned to read Latin, Greek, German, and French.

Dates in Helen Keller's Life

1880—Helen is born in Tuscumbia, Alabama on June 27.

1882—Helen becomes ill at 19 months, losing her sight and hearing.

1887—Helen meets Anne Sullivan, her teacher.

1888—Helen and Anne go to the Perkins School for the Blind.

1900—Helen enters Radcliffe College.

1904—Helen graduates from Radcliffe College.

1918—Helen stars in a movie about her life.

1920–1924—Helen, Anne, and Polly perform on stage.

1936—Anne Sullivan dies.

1943–1946—Helen visits soldiers wounded during World War II.

1964—Helen is awarded the Presidential Medal of Freedom.

1968—Helen dies on June 1.

Words to Know

activist (AK-ti-visst)—a person who works for changes in laws

aide (AYD)—a helper or an assistant

communicate (kuh-MYOO-nuh-kate)—to share information, ideas, or feelings with another person; people communicate by talking, writing, and using sign language.

fever (FEE-vur)—a body temperature that is higher than normal

military (MIL-uh-ter-ee)—members of the armed forces

tantrum (TAN-truhm)—an outburst of anger

Read More

Lakin, Patricia. *Helen Keller and the Big Storm.* Childhood of Famous Americans. New York: Aladdin, 2002.

Sutcliffe, Jane. *Helen Keller.* On My Own Biography. Minneapolis: Carolrhoda Books, 2002.

Walker, Pamela. *Helen Keller.* Real People. New York: Children's Press, 2001.

Useful Addresses

**American Foundation for
the Blind**
11 Penn Plaza
Suite 300
New York, NY 10001

Ivy Green
300 West North Commons
Tuscumbia, AL 35674

Internet Sites

Track down many sites about Helen Keller.
Visit the FACT HOUND at *http://www.facthound.com*

IT IS EASY! IT IS FUN!

1) Go to *http://www.facthound.com*
2) Type in: 0736816054
3) Click on "FETCH IT" and FACTHOUND will
   find several links hand-picked by our editors.

Relax and let our pal FACT HOUND do the research for you!

Index